LOOK!

THE ULTIMATE SPOT~THE~DIFFERENCE

Illustrated by APRIL WILSON

Nature notes by A . J . WOOD

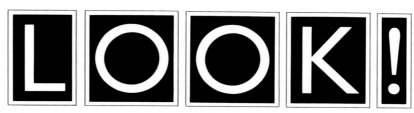

CHARLES LETTS · *Letts* · FOUNDED 1796

For my family – A.W.

A TEMPLAR BOOK

First published 1990 by Charles Letts & Co Ltd,
Diary House, Borough Road,
London SE1 1DW.

Devised and produced by The Templar Company plc,
Pippbrook Mill, London Road, Dorking, Surrey RH4 1JE, Great Britain.

Copyright © 1990 by The Templar Company plc

Researched by Rachael Kent
Designed by Mike Jolley
Colour separations by Positive Colour, Maldon, Essex, Great Britain.
Printed by L.E.G.O., Vicenza, Italy.

ISBN 1-85238-130-2

'LETTS' is a registered trademark of Charles Letts (Scotland) Ltd.

*F*rom the flooded forests of the Amazon to the dusty plains of the African savanna, the depths of the Indo-Pacific ocean to the snows of Japan's volcanic mountains, the following pages illustrate some of the Earth's diverse natural habitats.

Each page and its partner are seemingly identical. Closer inspection of each pair will reveal twelve vital differences – the great green tree frog will have caught its insect meal, a tiny hummingbird may have appeared on a branch, or a stray leaf fallen to lie on the lazy waters of a tropical river.

If you're tired of looking, turn to the back of the book and all will be revealed. You'll also find a fascinating guide to the wonders of the natural world contained within each colourful plate.

HOW TO USE THIS BOOK

At the back of the book you will find a key to the contents of each colour plate. The twelve "differences" are highlighted in red. In some cases, one difference may involve several additions to the picture – more than one baby sea horse may have appeared, for example. In such cases, only one of these additions will be highlighted and these changes will only count as one out of the twelve to be discovered. All the various plant and animal species contained within the picture are also numbered in accordance with the guide that follows.

Flora and fauna of Northern Europe

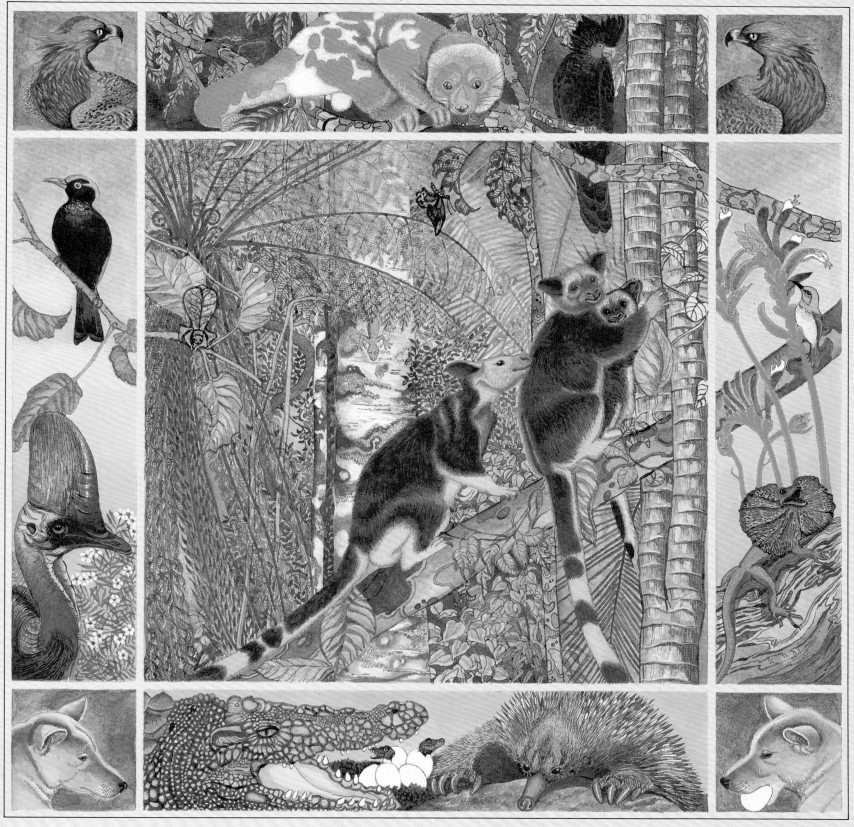

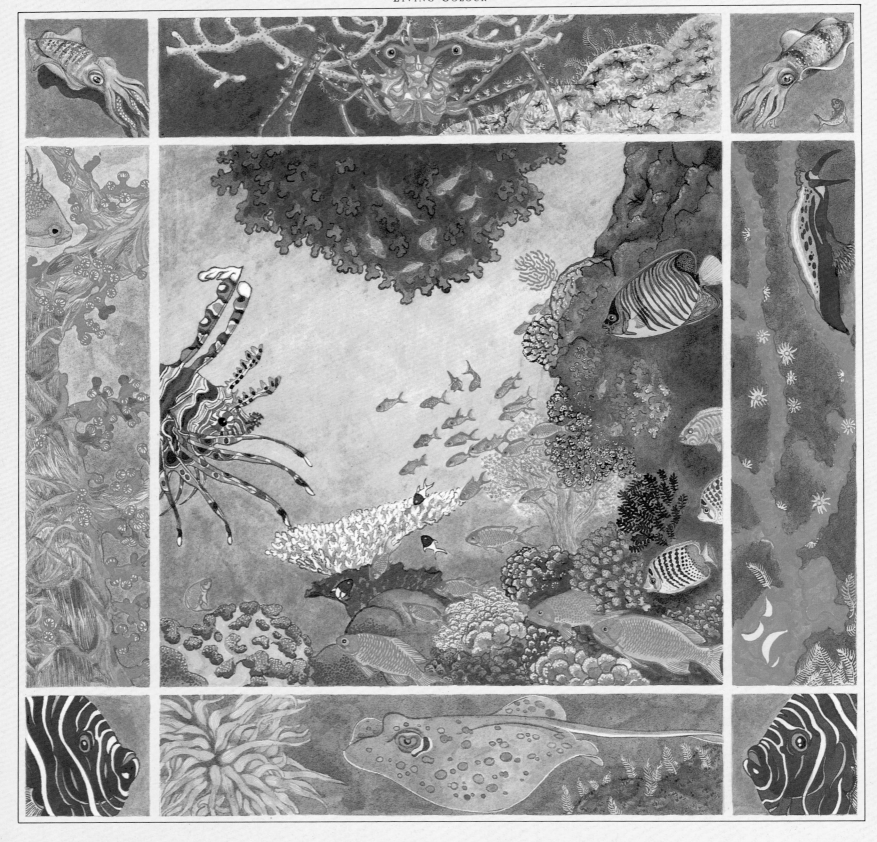

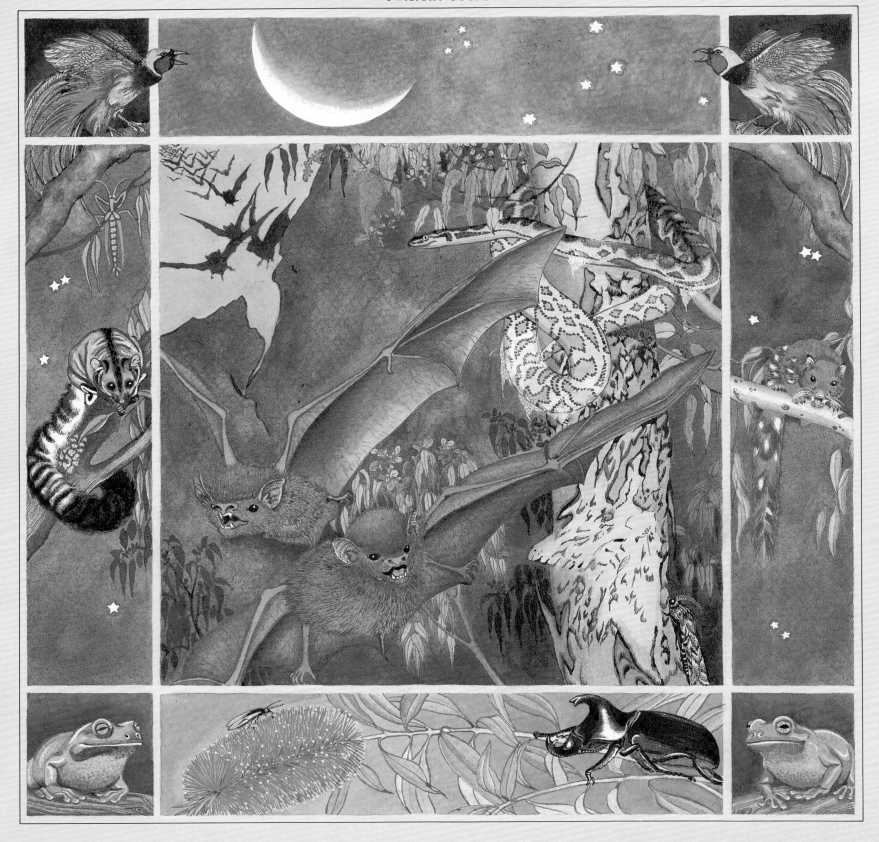

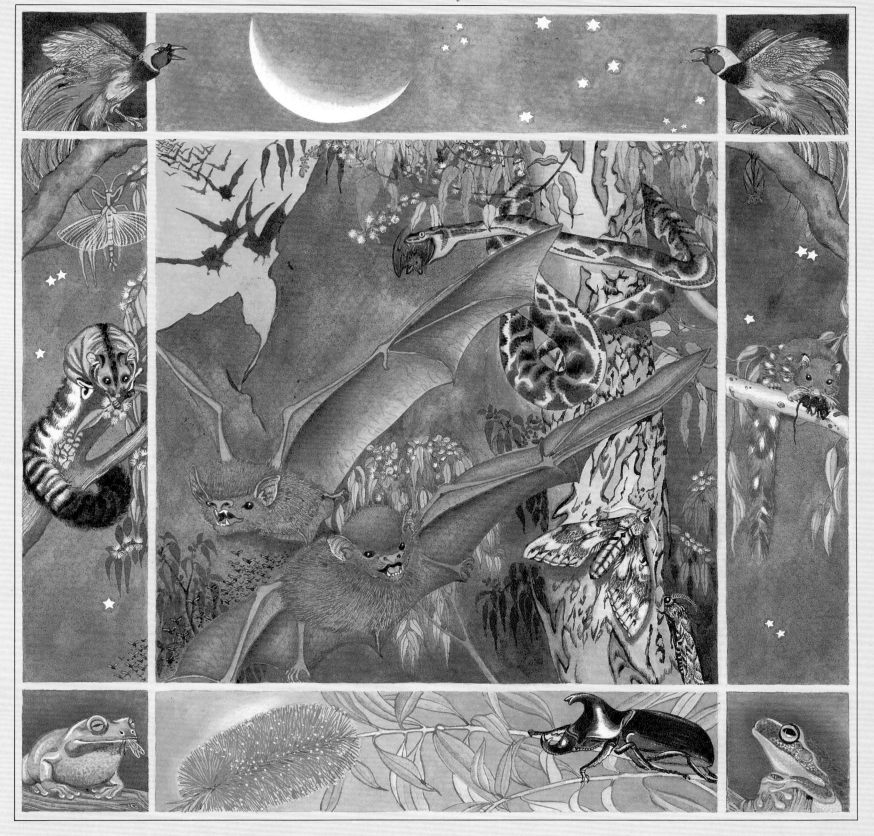

Flora and fauna of Mexico

RIVER'S EDGE
Flora and fauna of South Asia

*M*any creatures congregate at the river's edge – forest-dwellers, migrating birds, and inhabitants of the dry grassland in search of life-giving water. From the sacred gavial to the majestic tiger, the sly python to the impressive egret, many forms of life await the observant eye.

1. Leopard – The distinctive markings of the leopard provide camouflage among the trees and grassland where it stalks its prey. Colour mutations sometimes occur such as the black form, or panther.

2. Flying lemur – Despite its name, this living parachute is unrelated to the true lemurs. This creature can glide up to 130 metres using the membrane of skin which extends down both sides of its body.

3. Banana – The tip of this banana plant bears a single male flower. Further up are the clusters of female flowers which lose their petals and develop into fruits without being fertilized.

4. Indian python – These snakes kill their prey by constriction, wrapping themselves around the body of their victim so tightly that it cannot breathe.

5. Polyura butterfly – The male of this brightly-coloured species is often territorial and aggressive.

6. Pepper vine – The berry-like fruits of the pepper vine ripen from green to red and are harvested as peppercorns.

7. Leaf butterfly – When at rest this insect has a leaf-like appearance.

8. Golden oriole – These forest-dwellers migrate to Europe during the summer.

9. Bengal tigers – Now under threat of extinction, the tiger was once widespread over the whole of Eurasia. Rare mutations known as white tigers have been known, having lighter coats but the same distinctive pattern of dark stripes, designed to camouflage them amongst the undergrowth.

10. Gavial – Related to the crocodile, this long-snouted reptile sweeps its sharp-toothed jaws from side to side in an effort to catch fish. It is sacred to the Hindu.

11. Gliding frogs – These frogs do not take to water when breeding but lay their eggs in foam nests made among large leaves.

12. Plumed egret – Like other herons, egrets frequent pools, rivers and marshes, feeding or roosting in flocks.

13. Mango plant – A member of the cashew family, the mango is one of the most widely cultivated fruits of the tropical world.

14. Argus pheasant – By raising his wing feathers to form a huge fan, the male of this species hopes to attract a mate.

SNOWY FOOTHILLS
Flora and fauna of Northern Europe

*O*nce common across a far greater range of the continent, much of Europe's more exotic wildlife is now confined to its remaining areas of wilderness. Only a few species, such as the ubiquitous fox, have adapted to live alongside the human race – equally at home in city alley or forest glade.

1. Reed warbler nest – Along with some other insect-eating birds, the reed warbler is often the unwitting host to an egg laid by the parasitic cuckoo. Always similar in colour to its bed-fellows, this larger egg soon hatches. The young cuckoo quickly pushes out the other eggs or young to be exclusively looked after by its foster parents.

2. Bumble bees and bee orchis – Disputedly named after the appearance of its flowerheads, the bee orchis is regularly visited by bumble bees and other insects in their search for nectar and pollen.

3. Magpie moth and caterpillar – This is one of the few moths to share the same colouration as its caterpillar.

4. Barn owl – The diet of the barn owl consists mainly of rodents and small birds. Owls cannot digest feathers, fur or bones, and regurgitate this waste matter as pellets.

5. Long eared bat – Unlike most other species of bat, this night-time hunter can walk and climb with relative ease.

6. Hawk moth – Unlike butterflies, moths fly commonly at night, popular prey to bats.

7. Red deer – Also known as the wapiti, the handsome stags of this species indulge in fierce, antler-crashing fights in autumn.

8. Red fox – A versatile and intelligent animal, the red fox preys on large rodents but will eat fruit and berries in autumn.

9. Guelder rose – This small tree or shrub provides valuable food for wildlife in winter with its showy bunches of berries.

10. Lynx – A solitary animal, the lynx will use its keen senses to follow scent trails in relentless pursuit of its prey.

11. Greater spotted woodpecker – This bird drills or prises insects from tree bark.

12. Wild boar – Except for old males which are solitary, these ancestors of the domestic pig live in groups. The males have sharp tusks and can be dangerous if alarmed. The young lose their stripes when mature.

13. Stoat – In winter, the reddish-brown fur of the stoat turns white, camouflaging it against the snow-covered ground.

14. Otters – The elusive otter is well adapted for life in the water. It has webbed feet and dense fur which traps air to keep its skin permanently dry.

15. Adders – This is one of the few species of snake where males and females are different colours – females being browner.

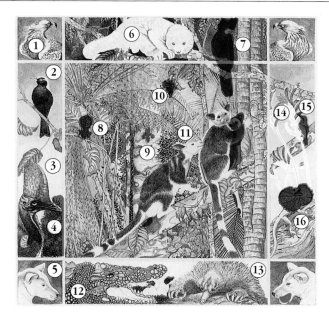

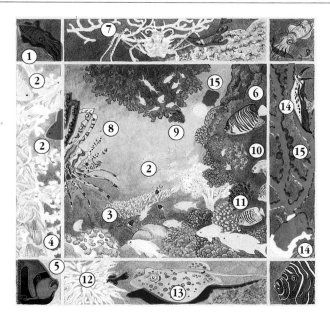

A FOREST OF FERNS
The rainforests of Australia and New Guinea

*M*any of the "trees" of the Australasian rainforests are, in fact, ferns, towering to some 25 metres in height. They are living fossils, growing to the same basic design as their ancestors – the ferns that formed the great forests of the Carboniferous period some 345 million years ago.

1. Wedge-tailed eagle – Australia's largest eagle, capable of killing an adult dingo, although smaller prey is most usually taken.

2. Regent bowerbird – The elaborate entrance to this bird's nest, or bower, is adorned with flowers, berries, feathers, and even shells.

3. Cassowary – These large, flightless birds are crowned with a bony helmet or casque. They are rarely seen, skulking in dense undergrowth and rapidly making for cover if surprised.

4. Waxplant – This shrub has aromatic leaves and stiff, wax-like flowers.

5. Dingo – The wild dog of Australia, the dingo is a scavenger as well as a hunter and will eat birds' eggs as well as meat.

6. Spotted phalanger – Largest of the possums, the phalanger or cuscus is a slow-moving, sluggish animal which rests, curled up in dense foliage, by day.

7. Cockatoo – Easily distinguished by their tufted crest, the plumage of cockatoos varies from white, pink and yellow to black.

8. Leaf insect – Like others of the stick insect family, this creature mimics the foliage on which it sits.

9. Gecko – This remarkable lizard can cling to any surface, with the help of microscopic hooks that cover the surface of its toe pads.

10. Birdwing butterfly – The graceful forewings of this insect may span more than 25 centimetres across.

11. Tree kangaroos – These shy relatives of the land wallaby have adapted to a tree-dwelling life and are seldom seen.

12. Crocodile – Female crocodiles may lay over 100 eggs in a covered nest. The young begin to grunt before hatching – a signal to the mother to uncover them.

13. Echidna – Also known as the spiny anteater, this monotreme lays a single egg which is incubated in a pouch on the mother's belly.

14. Kangaroo paws – These tropical plants are named after the appearance of their unopened buds.

15. Honeyeater – These songbirds have specialized tongues with brush-like tips for picking up pollen and insects.

16. Frilled lizard – A so-called dragon of Australia, this lizard will gape and unfurl its frill to frighten predators.

LIVING COLOUR
Life in the Red Sea

*T*he long, narrow arm of the Red Sea, sheltered between the great land masses of Africa and Asia, is home to one of the most impressive and vulnerable marine habitats. The rainbow forest of its coral reef is alive with colour – from the shoals of brilliantly-patterned fish to the curiously incandescent squid.

1. Squid – A master of colour change, the light-emitting squid can contract and expand its skin to produce a variety of patterns and hues. Fish and crustaceans are paralysed with venom produced by the squid's salivary glands before being eaten.

2. Fairy basslets – These brilliant orange fish may change sex during their lifetime – from pale orange female to darker male.

3/4. Corals – These "flower animals", the individual coral polyp, usually live in huge colonies. The stony corals (3) have hard external skeletons, generations of which build up to form reefs. The soft corals (4) are jelly-like. Both open the delicate tentacles around their mouths to catch food.

5/6. Angelfish – These beautiful fish use their bright colour to advertise possession of their territory and warn off intruders. The colour of the young imperial angelfish (5) changes from blue and white to blue and yellow as it matures. The king angelfish (6) displays a similar diversity of colour and marking with age.

7. Decorator crab – This curious creature literally decorates its body with pieces of the sea fan among which it lives.

8. Tigerfish – The striking markings and long poisonous spines of this fish act as a warning to any would-be predator.

9. Grouper – These fish are carnivorous and have strong jaws armed with many needle-like teeth. They can grow to 3 metres in length.

10. Wrasse – The many species of wrasse are noted for their brilliant colours which, unusually, differ greatly between sexes.

11. Butterflyfish – An agile swimmer, the butterflyfish flutters around the reef, diving into cracks and crevices if alarmed.

12. Sea anemone and boxfish – The boxfish finds danger among the anemone's stinging tentacles.

13. Blue-spotted ray – Also known as the ribbontail, this fish will lash out with its venomous tail spines if disturbed.

14. Sea slugs – The sea slugs include some of the most brightly-coloured sea animals. The body of the red hexauranchus is masked by a white mantle which spreads out like the petals of an exotic flower.

15. Sea fan – A gorgonian or soft coral, this colourful sea creature has a fan-like, flattened growth.

THE DUSTY PLAINS
The grasslands of the African savanna

*T*he tropical grasslands of the African savanna stretch in an almost unbroken band across southern Africa, from the Atlantic to the Indian Ocean. Dominated by tall grasses and low, flat-topped trees, these dusty plains are home to both the hunter and the hunted.

1. African tulip tree – Aptly known also as flame of the forest, this tree has brilliant scarlet blossom.

2/3. Weaverbirds – Compulsive nest builders, the male village weaverbird (2) exhibits brightly-coloured plumage in the breeding season. Many birds will live together in one tree, their nests hanging like strange fruit from the branches. The red bishop (3) is also a member of the weaver family.

4. Aloe flowers – Related to the lilies, these succulent plants can grow to over 2 metres in height. Many have brilliant blossoms.

5. Blackheaded oriole – These birds are accomplished mimics and will search vegetation in their hunt for insects.

6. Warthog – Inoffensive to everything but the eye, the warthog is quite capable of fighting off the most ferocious predator but does not develop tusks until maturity.

7. Blue–naped mousebird – These birds run along branches in the same manner as a rodent, holding their tail and body horizontal, hence their name.

8. Swallowtail butterflies – These insects often congregate at the edge of water holes to feed on salts left in the sand by the urine of grazing animals.

9. Burchell's zebras – Of the three species of zebra, this is the most common, distinguished from the others by the size and extent of its stripes.

10. Oxpecker – Often seen perching on the back of grazing animals, these birds feed on the flies and ticks of their host.

11. Ground squirrel – This squirrel finds refuge in burrows dug into the ground where it will hoard a cache of seeds, nuts and grain.

12. Acacias – Known in Africa as thorns, these trees provide prickly food to grazing animals such as the giraffe.

13. Mimosa – Related to the acacia, these trees have feathery leaves and carry their flowers in round, yellow catkins.

14. Boomslang – A deadly poisonous snake, the boomslang can slide to the tip of the most slender branch. It can remain so motionless that its prey of birds will even use it as a perch.

15. Golden pipit – Although often seen perching in the very tops of trees, these birds nest on the ground.

THE FLOODED FOREST
The rainforests of the Amazon

*R*ising in the mountains of Peru, the mighty Amazon flows some 4,000 miles to enter the Atlantic in northern Brazil, and is covered for most of its length by a green mantle of rainforest. Always threatened by destruction, it is home to many jewels of the natural world – personifying paradise, sometimes even in name.

1. Night monkey – Often referred to as the owl monkey, this is the only monkey that is active mainly at night.

2. Coatimundi – This small carnivorous mammal is related to the raccoon.

3. Three-toed sloth – These curious creatures are totally adapted to a tree-dwelling life, mostly spent hanging upside-down. Their coats encourage the growth of algae, giving them a greenish tinge which provides camouflage among the foliage.

4. Heliconia plant – The claw-shaped, bright scarlet bracts of this tropical plant give it its common name of lobster-claws.

5. Ocelot – One of the most beautiful and secretive members of the cat family, the ocelot is mainly nocturnal. Often hunting in pairs, the two partners mew continually to keep in touch in the darkness.

6. Passionflower – This plant is an impressive climber thanks to its long, curling tendrils. Its showy flowers produce fleshy orange fruits, edible in some species.

7. Jaguar – Lying in wait on an overhanging branch, this splendid creature sometimes dips its tail into the water to act as a lure for fish, flipping out the unsuspecting victim with a single strike of its paw. Mammals, birds, and turtles are also eaten.

8. Morphinae butterflies – These flying jewels of the forest will spread their brilliant blue wings to the sun, the undersides of which are marked with "eyes" or ocelli.

9. Rainbow boa – The skin of this snake has an iridescent sheen, caused by the reflection of ultra-violet light from its scales.

10. Arapaima fish – The largest freshwater fish in the world, the arapaima may reach 4 metres in length. It is only ever found in the murky waters of the Amazon Basin.

11. Paradise tanager – Primarily a fruit-eater, this beautiful relative of the honey-creeper forages amongst the trees for berries, insects and spiders. It may raid wasps' nests hunting for larvae and pupae.

12. Purple honeycreeper – These brightly-coloured birds suck nectar from flowers with their long, curved bills.

13. Macaws – The largest and most spectacular members of the parrot family, these birds are often found in screeching flocks. Both the scarlet and the gold and blue macaws are threatened by the destruction of their habitat.

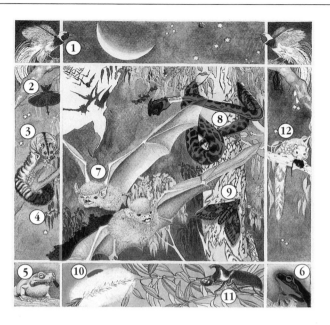

FIRE AND ICE
The volcanic springs of Japan

*H*igh above the bustling cities, their skyline dominated only by Mount Fuji itself, are the bubbling springs of Japan's volcanic mountains. Their offer of warmth among the snow and ice provides an unusual resting place for many of Japan's rare and beautiful creatures.

1. Sika deer – Native to Japan, the Sika or Japanese deer was introduced to the West by the gift of a stag and three hinds from the Emperor of Japan to a French dignitary in the 1800s. As with all true deer, males carry antlers which are shed each year, growing from simple, velvety stumps to slender antlers with eight points, or tines.

2. Northern goshawks – During the nesting period, the female remains in the nest while the male brings food, leaving it on a nearby perch for her to collect.

3. Ginkgo tree – Also known as the maidenhair tree, the gingko is the only living representative of a tree family that first appeared in the Carboniferous period.

4. Bamboo – This tall, tree-like grass forms dense forests, with a hundred columns or stems springing from a single plant. The growth rate of bamboo is perhaps one of its most impressive features – some species growing as much as 50 centimetres in a day.

5. Asiatic black bear – Also known as the crescent-moon bear because of the white markings on its chest, this impressive animal is mainly vegetarian, feeding on berries, nuts, seeds, and honey.

6. Japanese cranes – The Japanese or Manchurian crane is one of the rarest birds in the world. During the breeding season, these birds indulge in a spectacular dance, strutting around with wings half spread.

7. Japanese macaques – The only monkey found in Japan, the macaque is the sole primate apart from man that can live in near-freezing temperatures. It makes use of the volcanic springs that occur in some parts of its habitat by bathing in the steaming waters. The dark fur of the young lightens with age, and females remain close to their mothers throughout their lives.

8. Cherry blossom – A springtime image of Japan known worldwide, the blossom of the cherry tree comes in clusters of white or pink flowers.

9. White-eye – Flocks of these birds forage among trees, searching for nectar, berries, and insects. Their name comes from the white rings around their eyes.

10. Admiral butterfly – Named after its wing bands which resemble a naval uniform, the brown underside of this insect provides instant camouflage when the wings are closed.

TWILIGHT SOUND
The mountain scrub of Australasia

*A*s dusk falls and the first stars of the Southern Cross light up the night sky, the air is filled with sounds of life. From the fluttering of a hundred bats out on a nocturnal hunt for food, to the croaking of a solitary tree frog searching for a mate, a rich diversity of life makes itself known.

1. Bird of paradise – During the breeding season, the male of the species performs an elaborate courtship dance to attract the female, fluffing out his tail into a long, lacy cascade of red plumes.

2. Stick insect – The longest living insects, these strange creatures can remain motionless for hours at a time, imitating the vegetation on which they sit. Some species may exceed 30 centimetres in length.

3. Sugar glider – Sometimes called flying squirrels, these marsupials have a gliding membrane between their fore and hind limbs enabling them to "fly" from tree to tree.

4. Eucalyptus – These fast-growing, drought-resistant trees are commonly known as gums or stringy-barks. Their showy flowers have only tiny petals but a mass of fluffy stamens.

5/6. Tree frogs – These agile frogs feed on insects, often seized in the air during a flying leap. There are many species – such as the great green (5) and orange-eyed (6) forms shown here. All have sticky pads on their feet that enable them to cling to leaves and branches.

7. Bentwing bats – The only mammals capable of true flight, bats hunt for food at night, using echolocation to track down their insect food. Most species spend the day sleeping, suspended upside-down from branches or in caves.

8. Children's python – Agile climbers, these snakes grow throughout their lives, periodically shedding their old skin which becomes opaque before peeling off. All species can dislocate their jaws, enabling them to capture and swallow creatures much larger than themselves.

9. Wood moth – An expert at camouflage, the wing span of this moth may reach 25 centimetres or more.

10. Bottlebrush – Named after the appearance of its colourful flowerheads, this evergreen shrub provides food for many insects, including the thynninae wasp shown here.

11. Rhinoceros beetle – Aptly named because of its huge horn, this beetle can reach 15 centimetres in length.

12. Spotted quoll – This marsupial cat is largely nocturnal, feeding on small vertebrates such as lizards and mice.

DESERT LIFE
Flora and fauna of Mexico

A selection of colourful creatures gathers around a trickle of water at the edge of Mexico's Sonoran Desert. A startling quetzal looks down from the branch of a nearby tree, its name a reminder of Mexico's distant past – when Montezuma ruled his Aztec empire, last in a line of ancient races to rule an ancient land.

1. Raccoon – A solitary animal, the raccoon eats a wide variety of plant and animal food, from frogs to fruit, roots to rodents.

2. Fishing buzzard – This hawk has tiny spines on the underside of its toes to help it catch and hold its prey of fish.

3. Ruby-throated hummingbird – Despite its size, at only 9 centimetres long, this diminutive bird migrates over 500 miles across the Gulf of Mexico each year, from the eastern USA to its wintering grounds.

4. Axolotl – This curious salamander derives its name from the Aztec word meaning "water monster". Most individuals never progress beyond the larval stage, remaining all their lives underwater. Some do metamorphose, lose their gills, and become land-dwelling adults.

5. Gila monster – This poisonous lizard tracks down its prey by smell, using its tongue to pick up tiny scent particles.

6. Monarch butterflies – Every autumn these insects fly southward from the USA in huge swarms, passing the winter in a state of semi-hibernation before beginning their journey northward in the spring.

7. Puma – Also known as the cougar or mountain lion, this cat is a powerful hunter and can jump 6 metres in a single bound.

8. Striped skunks – When attacked, the skunk will squirt a foul-smelling fluid at its enemy which can temporarily halt breathing.

9. Prickly pears – These flat-stemmed, spiky cacti produce yellow, orange and red flowers, and edible, pear-shaped fruit.

10. Coral snake – The striking colours of the poisonous coral snake warn away potential attackers.

11. Bobwhite – A member of the quail family, this gregarious bird is named in imitation of its call.

12. Tiger salamanders – Up to 40 centimetres in length, this is the largest land-dwelling salamander. Its colour and pattern varies as greatly as its diet which includes worms, mice, and other amphibians.

13. Quetzal – The tail feathers of this bird may reach 60 centimetres and were highly prized by the Aztecs. The bird itself was considered sacred and its name given to the plumed serpent god Quetzalcoatl.

14. Coppery-tailed trogon – This bird is rarely seen on the ground and will perch, motionless, on a branch for long periods.

OCEAN DEEP
The Indo-Pacific Ocean

In the deep, clear waters of the Indo-Pacific an extraordinary selection of creatures can be found. There is no conformity of shape here, and much is not as it first appears. Bizarre plant forms are revealed to be strange sea creatures, and amongst the rocks lurk a deadly array of well-camouflaged predators.

1. Nautilus – Similar in design to its ancestral relative, the ammonite, this cephalopod catches its prey in tentacles surrounding its beak-like mouth.

2. Triggerfish – These fish will take refuge in a rock crevice when alarmed, wedging themselves in with the aid of their strong dorsal spine.

3. Filefish – Relatives of the triggerfish, these fish are rough to the touch, hence their name.

4. Clams – These molluscs may reach more than a metre across. Smaller varieties are prey to starfish who will prise open the shell with their tube-feet.

5. Brittle-star – Unlike starfish, these animals move by using rowing movements of their arms.

6. Sea slugs – These vividly coloured sea animals have exotic flaps and folds which increase their body surface for respiration.

7. Green turtle – The green, or edible, turtle breeds only once a year, the females coming ashore to lay their eggs.

8/9. Cleaner fish feeding on grunt fish – As their name suggests, cleaners feed on the external parasites living on their host.

10. Sea dragon – Looking surprisingly like seaweed thanks to the many flaps of skin attached to its body, this sea horse hatches its young from fertilized eggs deposited in a pouch on the male's belly.

11. Blue-ringed octopus – When alarmed, this ruthless hunter will change colour and posture to accentuate its blue rings. Females lay about 150,000 eggs which are attached in long strands about the entrance to the mother's lair. Each egg is smaller than a grain of rice.

12. Moray eel – A monster of the deep, the moray will hide, concealed amongst the rocks, and then strike out – seizing its prey with strong jaws.

13. Crinoid – Also known as featherstars, these marine animals are related to starfish.

14. Cling fish – Also known as suckers, the pelvic fins of these fish form a suction pad, hence their name.

15. Spotted crabs – Camouflaged amongst the rocks, like all crabs this species will swim or scuttle sideways to escape a predator.

16. Sea pen – This relative of the corals produces a luminous fluid when touched.

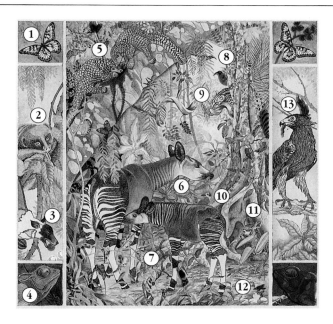

UNDER THE EAGLE'S EYE
The foothills of the Rocky Mountains

S tretching in an unbroken line from New Mexico to the Yukon, the chief mountain range of North America rises up from the central plains, once home to many tribes of North American Indians. Now partly a National Park, this wilderness is the haunt of the eagle and the bear, the coyote and the rattlesnake.

1. Bald eagle – The national symbol of the USA, this impressive bird of prey is now a protected species. The impression of baldness is given by its snow-white head feathers which contrast sharply with the dark brown plumage of its body. These white feathers develop only once maturity is reached. Primarily a fish-eater, the bald eagle will include birds, small mammals, snakes, and carrion in its diet.

2. Coyote – A relative of the wolf and part-ancestor of the domestic dog, coyotes often hunt in pairs – one taking up the chase as the other tires. Despite being trapped and poisoned by man the coyote continues to thrive and has a wide-ranging diet that includes rabbits, snakes, fruit, fish, and even crustaceans.

3. Moose – The moose or elk is the largest living deer. The males have massive antlers which grow each year and are at first covered with a layer of skin or velvet. Once the antlers are fully grown, the velvet dries and is rubbed off.

4. Mustangs – The ancestor of the horse – eohippus – is thought to have originated in North America, yet the wild horse or mustang found there today is believed to have descended from the stock of Spanish settlers. The black and white piebald and the brown and white skewbald varieties are often referred to as "pintos" from the Spanish word meaning painted. These wild horses, along with the speckled Appaloosa, were highly prized by the American Indians.

5. Scrub pine – These low-growing conifers provide a prickly refuge for many nesting birds.

6. Timber rattlesnake – Typically, the timber rattlesnake has a "rattle" at the end of its tail, formed of hollow, horny segments. These make a noise when shaken and act as a warning to potential enemies that the snake is about to strike.

7. Grizzly bear – The cubs of this bear are born at the end of their mother's winter sleep. They are almost hairless, blind, and toothless at birth. Agile climbers when young, these bears lose the ability with age, mainly due to their great size and weight.

8. Yellow poppy – These fragile flowers produce many hundreds of tiny seeds which can lay dormant in the earth for centuries before germination takes place.

HIDING IN THE JUNGLE
The rainforests of Central Africa

I n 1874 Sir Henry Morton Stanley first set eyes on Africa's dense jungle, when travelling down the Congo (now Zaire) River after his famous encounter with Dr Livingstone. Many of the creatures that live there are shy, timid animals, using camouflage to keep themselves hidden among the impenetrable undergrowth.

1. Eupaedia butterflies – The iridescent wings of these splendid butterflies catch the light as they fly through the tangle of vegetation, looking for a suitable place to lay their eggs.

2. Potto – A slow mover, the potto only moves one limb at a time, gripping the branches with its vice-like feet.

3. Fruit bat – Feeding mainly on fruit and nectar, this bat will fill its cheek pouches and fly to a convenient perch to eat.

4. Chameleons – Young chameleons are independent almost from birth - although they may be eaten by a hungry parent! All species are masters of colour change, matching their skin colour to that of their immediate surroundings.

5. Pangolins – These armoured mammals are also known as scaly anteaters. Despite their appearance, they are agile climbers, searching the branches for insect food.

6. Okapis – Undiscovered until 1901, this relative of the giraffe has a striped coat which makes it hard to spot when standing motionless in the shadows.

7. Egg-eating snake – Unlike many other snakes, this species lives almost exclusively on eggs, seeking them out by their smell.

8. Bee-eaters – Easily spotted because of their colourful plumage, these birds will often be found in flocks. They nest in burrows, dug into soft earth.

9. Genet – Related to both the cat and weasel family, genets are solitary, nocturnal hunters. Their pale facial markings are used for recognition in the gloom of the forest.

10. Bare-headed rock fowl – This flightless bird is also known as the babbler because of its loud, continuous cry.

11. Bongo fawn – Like the okapi, the bongo has a camouflaged coat. The adults have spirally twisted horns.

12. Soft-shelled turtles – These turtles have a leathery coating to their shells. They lay between 10 and 25 eggs in shallow holes in the ground. The young head for fresh water as soon as they hatch, but frequently fall prey to snakes.

13. Long-crested eagle – This majestic bird of prey feeds on small mammals, birds and reptiles, and gains its name from the crest of feathers on its head which are raised in display.